KNOW JUSTICE
KNOW PEACE
LEADER'S GUIDE

UP Uriel Press

A DIVISION OF UMI

Scripture quotations are from the New King James Version Bible, English Standard Version Bible, The Message Version Bible, The Good News Translation Bible, and New International Version Bible.

Published in the United States by Uriel Press
P.O. Box 436987, Chicago, IL 60643
www.urielpress.com

ISBN: 979-8-9933670-0-2 (paperback)

Cover design by Laura Duffy

Printed in the United States of America

Contents

Leader's Guide Instructions. v

Getting Started vi

Introduction viii

Chapter Summaries 1

   1. Know Justice, Know Peace. 2

   2. Know Justice, Know the Scriptures 4

   3. Know Justice, Know Restoration. 7

   4. Know Justice, Like Waters 9

      a. Justice Like Waters 11

   5. Knowing The Human Heart. 12

      a. The Human Heart. 13

   6. Knowing The Ways of the Unjust. 16

   7. Knowing God's Justice. 18

   8. Knowing How to Walk Your Justice 21

   9. Knowing True Worship 26

  10. Knowing The Way to Worship God. 29

  11. Knowing How to Impress God. 31

  12. Knowing The Price of Pride. 33

  13. Knowing My Pain. 37

  14. Knowing The Injustice of Man. 39

  15. Knowing Injustice 42

  16. Knowing What To Do 45

17. Knowing Outrage 48

18. Knowing The Plan of God 50

19. Knowing Biblical Justice in Society 53

20. Knowing Biblical Justice and the Laws 56

21. Knowing God's Answer to Discrimination 59

22. Know How to Love Mercy 62

23. Knowing Justice in Society 65

24. Knowing Justice and the Church 68

25. Knowing Equity 71

26. Knowing How to Be Like God 73

27. Knowing Justice in the Power of the Cross 75

28. Knowing Crisis Response 77

    Bibliography 79

    Disclaimer 80

    Systematic Bible Study Section 81

    Purpose of the Study Guide 83

    Definition of Systematic Theology 84

    Justice in the Bible 86

    Key Attributes of God: Justice 88

    Summary 90

Leader's Guide Instructions

The Leader's Guide is designed to facilitate a study on justice. It summarizes the key points and provides discussion prompts for each of the 28 chapters.

As the Discussion Leader, you should review the scriptures identified in each possible answer. Then lead the participants to understand the major focal points. The content of this guide is designed to help leaders direct participants to a deeper understanding of biblical justice.

Getting Started

Welcome to the *Know Justice, Know Peace* Bible study experience. This Leader's Guide/Workbook provides a biblical perspective on justice, rooted in God's character and His will for His people. Have you ever wondered why the justice journey and the important role of God's people in addressing injustice are seldom discussed in the church or Bible colleges? Could it be that our land remains in need of healing because God's people shy away from seeking His face on this issue (2 Chronicles 7:14)? Are we capable of discerning between God's justice and our biases? Approaching justice from God's perspective allows us to face this issue without fear, inviting more power, love, and sound minds (2 Timothy 1:7). Expect healing and deliverance from misunderstanding what God's Word says about justice (Proverbs 4:7).

I am confident God is pleased with your decision to challenge yourself through individual study or enlighten others through small groups, congregational sermons, Bible college curriculum, or online conversations. Expect to hear from God and receive revelation and insight!

The scriptures in this workbook are curated to invoke thoughtful reflections on justice, injustice, the heart of God, and our role as His people. Each chapter contains questions to promote self-reflection or healthy dialogue. Be prayerful in discerning the difference between biblical justice and human perspectives.

Here are tips for maximizing your experience:

If studying individually, work at your own pace, but set a consistent schedule. Use the workbook as a daily devotion or a weekly chapter study. Write out your reflections and consider sharing insights on social media.

If facilitating a small group, work through the content prior to sessions and encourage each participant to have their own workbook. Establish an environment of respect and engagement. Allocate time for content discussion, activities, and prayer while fitting your needs.

Example session timeline (60 minutes):

- Open in prayer (5 min)
- Main leader recaps prior week, volunteers share insights (15 min)
- Main leader introduces chapter topic, shares stories, reviews scriptures (30 min)
- Table talk – small group discussion (25 min)
- Summary and insights from volunteers (10 min)
- Assign homework and close in prayer (5 min)

Note: For a 14-week study, alternate chapters between in-class and homework.

As Bible college curriculum, integrate workbook content into college coursework. Assign essays on chapter topics with personal reflections and practical applications.

As sermon content, adapt chapter topics for congregational sermons or a sermon series.

Whichever method you choose, trust that God has life-changing revelation in store for you. Let your biblically-based justice journey begin!

Introduction

The tall, hulking black man stood curiously over the small robot, looking down as though mesmerized by the wheeled gadget. Drunk, he couldn't seem to figure it out or hear what "it" was saying to him. He had fallen asleep in someone's backyard before officers and a TV camera in a helicopter had located him. Awakened, he rolled onto his side revealing a pistol beneath him.

He pocketed the pistol during his robot encounter. He seemed to politely entertain the talk with the robot. He approached it, bending over to hear and speak. The drunken scene was far too funny just weeks after the killing of George Floyd in Minneapolis, but I could not contain my laughter. The conversation with the little robot finally led him to lay the gun down on the grass, make his way down the driveway, past a second robot, and compliantly into the arresting arms of law officers.

At least part of my glee, I'm sure, had to do with the favorable, less than brutal or deadly outcome of the encounter. Creative law enforcement had found a "dignified" way to encounter an American citizen!

The chant in every justice situation is "No justice -No Peace". we take it to a new level when we declare, "Know Justice-Know Peace". Enjoy leading and learning. Enjoy changing the world, one heart at a time.

Chapter Summaries

CHAPTER 1

Know Justice, Know Peace

- **Key Point:** *The importance of understanding God's heart concerning justice.*

- **Discussion Prompt:** *Why do you think justice is a significant theme in the Bible?*

- **Possible Answers:** *Justice is a significant theme in the Bible for several reasons:*

1. **God's Divine Nature***: Justice is a core attribute of God's character. The Bible often describes God as just and righteous, emphasizing that His actions and judgments are fair and equitable. For example, Deuteronomy 32:4 states, "He is the Rock, his works are perfect, and all his ways are just. A faithful God who does no wrong, upright and just is he."*

2. **The Bible's Moral Foundation***: The Bible provides a moral framework for human behavior, and justice is a key component of this framework. It calls for fair treatment of all individuals, protection of the vulnerable, and accountability for wrongdoing. This is evident in passages like Micah 6:8, which says, "He has shown you, O mortal, what is good. And what does the Lord require of you? To act justly and to love mercy and to walk humbly with your God."*

3. **Social Justice***: The Bible advocates for social justice, urging believers to care for the poor, the oppressed, and the marginalized. This theme is prevalent in the teachings of the prophets*

and in the ministry of Jesus. For instance, Isaiah 1:17 instructs, "Learn to do right; seek justice. Defend the oppressed. Take up the cause of the fatherless; plead the case of the widow."

These aspects highlight why justice is a central theme in the Bible, reflecting God's character, guiding moral conduct, advocating for social equity, promoting restoration, and offering an eternal hope.

KNOWING THE WORD OF GOD

In recent years, discussions and debates about justice have been prevalent. The Church has both upheld and ignored justice at times. This reflection seeks to understand God's heart concerning justice.

Does God care about Justice? (Yes or no) _____ If you answered "yes", why do you think God cares about justice?

_____

If you answered "no", why do you think God doesn't care about justice?

_____

Luke 11:42 ESV "But woe to you Pharisees! For you tithe mint and rue and every herb, and neglect justice and the love of God. These you ought to have done, without neglecting the others."

What do you think Jesus was saying in this verse?

_____

In what ways does the verse say that Christian's neglect justice?

_____

In what ways do Christian's neglect the "love of God"?

_____

CHAPTER 2

Know Justice, Know the Scriptures

- **Key Point:** Jesus' teachings on the greatest commandments and their relation to justice.

- **Discussion Prompt:** How do these commandments guide our actions towards justice?

- **Possible Answers:** Here are some of God's commandments related to justice and how they guide our actions:

COMMANDMENTS RELATED TO JUSTICE

1. Do Not Steal: Exodus 20:15 - "You shall not steal."

2. Do Not Bear False Witness: Exodus 20:16 - "You shall not give false testimony against your neighbor."

3. Love Your Neighbor: Leviticus 19:18 - "Love your neighbor as yourself."

4. Do Not Oppress: Exodus 22:21 - "Do not mistreat or oppress a foreigner, for you were foreigners in Egypt."

5. Fair Treatment: Deuteronomy 16:19-20 - "Do not pervert justice or show partiality. Follow justice and justice alone, so that you may live and possess the land the Lord your God is giving you."

HOW THESE COMMANDMENTS GUIDE OUR ACTIONS

1. **Integrity and Honesty**: By not stealing and not bearing false witness, we uphold

integrity and honesty in our dealings with others. This builds trust and fairness in our communities.

2. ***Compassion and Empathy****: Loving our neighbors as ourselves encourages us to act with compassion and empathy, ensuring that we treat others with the same respect and kindness we desire.*

3. ***Protection of the Vulnerable****: The commandment to not oppress foreigners reminds us to protect and support those who are vulnerable or marginalized, promoting social justice and equality.*

These commandments provide a moral foundation that guides us to act justly, promote fairness, and ensure the well-being of all individuals in society. They encourage us to create a just and equitable world, reflecting God's character and intentions for humanity.

In this passage of scripture Jesus answers a question which has challenged religious leaders for thousands of years:

Matt. 22:35-40 NKJV And one of them, a lawyer, asked him a question to test him. **36** "Teacher, which is the great commandment in the Law?" **37** And he said to him, "You shall love the Lord your God with all your heart and with all your soul and with all your mind. **38** This is the great and first commandment. **39** And a second is like it: You shall love your neighbor as yourself. **40** On these two commandments depend on all the Law and the Prophets."

When the leader asked Jesus for "one" greatest commandment, why do you think Jesus gave him two commandments?

_____

According to Jesus in Matthew 22:40, what is the significance of these two commandments in relation to all other commandments and teachings of the prophets?

_____

Isaiah 61:8 ESV "For I the Lord love justice; I hate robbery and wrong; I will faithfully give them their recompense, and I will make an everlasting covenant with them."

What do you think God means when He says, "I, the Lord love justice"?

_____

What does the Lord promise in terms of compensation for those wronged, according to Isaiah 61:8 ESV?

_____

Luke 4:18-19 ESV "The Spirit of the Lord is upon me, because he has anointed me to proclaim good news to the poor. He has sent me to proclaim liberty to the captives and recovering of sight to the blind, to set at liberty those who are oppressed, to proclaim the year of the Lord's favor."

The Lord Jesus made this bold proclamation when He introduced Himself in the synagogue as God's promised Christ. In this scripture, which He read from a prophetic book written 700 years before His birth at Bethlehem, He outlines His earthly mission.

He listed four reasons for His coming. What are they?

_____

CHAPTER 3

Know Justice, Know Restoration

- *Key Point:* Isaiah's prophetic ministry and the promise of blessings for those who commit to righteousness and justice.

- *Discussion Prompt:* What does it mean to be a "repairer of the breach" in today's context?

- *Possible Answers:* The phrase "repairer of the breach" comes from Isaiah 58:12, where it describes those who restore and rebuild what has been broken. In today's context, being a "repairer of the breach" can mean several things:

1. *Healing Divisions:* Working to mend social, racial, and political divides in our communities. This involves promoting understanding, empathy, and reconciliation among different groups.

2. *Advocating for Justice:* Standing up for the oppressed and marginalized, ensuring that their voices are heard, and their rights are protected. This can include activism, legal advocacy, and community organizing.

3. *Restoring Relationships:* Helping to heal broken relationships within families, friendships, and communities. This can involve mediation, counseling, and fostering open communication.

In essence, being a "repairer of the breach" today means actively working to heal and restore what is broken in our world, whether it's relationships, *communities, or the environment. It's about making a positive impact and bringing about lasting change.*

Isaiah 58:12 ESV And your ancient ruins shall be rebuilt, you shall raise the foundations of many generations, you shall be called the repairer of the breach, the restorer of streets to dwell in.

Isaiah's prophetic ministry spanned the reigns of multiple Judean kings during the 8th century BCE. This was a tumultuous time, with the Assyrian Empire being the dominant force threatening the smaller nations, including the kingdoms of Israel and Judah. After rebuking the people for their insincere religious practices, God, through Isaiah, promises blessings for those who genuinely commit to righteousness and justice.

What might this passage be saying to you and to your generation?

_____

What role does the verse describe in relation to "the foundations of many generations"?

_____

What might the "breach" in "repairer of the breach" symbolize in a broader modern-day context?

_____

What are the two titles given to the individual or group mentioned in the verse?

_____

Isaiah 58:12 ESV is set against a backdrop of national spiritual decline, external religiosity without sincere commitment, and looming external threats. How does Isaiah 58:12 emphasize restoration and rebuilding in its message?

_____

CHAPTER 4

Know Justice, Like Waters

- **Key Point:** *Amos' makes a demand for justice and condemns the treatment of the poor.*

- **Discussion Prompt:** *How can we ensure justice runs down like waters in our communities?*

- **Possible Answers:** *Ensuring justice flows like a mighty river in our communities is a noble and essential goal. Here are some ways we can work towards achieving this:*

1. **Education and Awareness:** *Educate community members about their rights and the importance of justice. Awareness campaigns can help people understand the significance of justice and how they can contribute to it.*

2. **Community Engagement:** *Encourage active participation in community activities and decision-making processes. When people are involved, they are more likely to advocate for justice and hold authorities accountable.*

3. **Support for Marginalized Groups:** *Provide support and resources to marginalized and vulnerable groups. This can include legal aid, social services, and economic opportunities to help them overcome systemic barriers.*

KNOWING THE HEART OF GOD

Amo 5:10-13 NKJV They hate the one who rebukes in the gate, and they abhor the one who speaks uprightly. Amo 5:11 Therefore, because you tread down the poor and take grain taxes from him, though you have built houses of hewn stone, yet you shall not dwell in them; You have planted pleasant vineyards, But you shall not drink wine from them. Amo 5:12 For I Know your manifold transgressions and your mighty sins: Afflicting the just *and* taking bribes; Diverting the poor *from justice* at the gate. Amo 5:13 Therefore the prudent keep silent at that time, for it *is* an evil time.

In these verses, Amos demands justice in the affairs of men. The prophet condemns the men of Israel for the brutal treatment of the poor.

What is it they do to the poor?

_____

The word "just" means law-abiding. What do they do to the "just"?

_____

Professor Paige H. Kelley wrote, "In ancient Israel, the court room was the open gate at the entrance to the walled city. There the elders of the city were seated as judges to rule on cases that were brought before them. (Amos 5:15; Ruth 4:1-12;) " Dr. Kelley wrote

"In Amos' day, the trials were always rigged. The judges took bribes. The word used here for bribe is derived from a root meaning to cover. A bribe is covering money or hush money; the righteous, the inno-cent was never acquitted in these courts, but were afflicted, that is treated as if they were guilty." "To turn aside the needy in the gate. "Simply means to deny them a fair trial. (In some cases, vigilantism, police or otherwise). All the while God has been a silent witness to these transactions "for I Know your manifold, transgressions, and your mighty sins…"[1]

Amo 5:24 But let justice run down like waters, And righteousness like a mighty stream.

Does this verse seem to teach that God wants justice to be permitted and plentiful?

_____ (Yes or No)

---

[1] denverjournal.denverseminary.edu and preach-ingsource.com

Why do you think God wants justice to be plentiful?

_____

JUSTICE, LIKE WATERS

Bell Hooks wrote," Without justice there can be no love."[2] Read the first 23 verses of Amos chapter 5.

How many times does Amos use the word justice?

_____

What does that seem to mean?

_____

How many times, in the 5th chapter, does Amos mention the poor?

_____

What might the poor have to do with justice?

_____

Is poverty usually a justice issue?

_____

What are some ways poverty could be a justice issue?

_____

Is it possible for religious people to get it wrong about God?

_____

How did God seem to feel about religion without justice?

_____

[2] azquotes.com and goodreads.com

CHAPTER 5

Knowing The Human Heart

- **Key Point:** *The deceitfulness of the human heart and its impact on justice.*

- **Discussion Prompt:** *How can we guard against the deceitfulness of our own hearts?*

- **Possible Answers:**

  1. **Self-Reflection and Prayer:** *Regularly examine your thoughts and motives through self-reflection and prayer. This helps in identifying any deceitful tendencies and seeking God›s guidance to overcome them.*

  2. **Accountability:** *Surround yourself with a community of trusted individuals who can provide honest feedback and hold you accountable. This can help in recognizing and correcting any deceitful behavior.*

  3. **Scripture Study:** *Immerse yourself in the study of scriptures. The Bible provides wisdom and guidance that can help in discerning the truth and aligning your heart with God›s will.*

  4. **Humility:** *Cultivate a humble attitude, acknowledging that we are all susceptible to deceit. This openness allows for growth and correction.*

THE DEPTH AND HEIGHTS OF THE HEART OF MAN

Amy Vaughan, an FBI intelligence analyst, was shocked to discover vulgar and hateful language from a seemingly regular citizen. Though she is white, the racist language repulsed her. Kristie Ronquille, a respected member of the U.S. Coast Guard, experienced similar attacks with hateful, racist language. She had dated a black basketball player and was called an 'n-word lover.' Both women testified at the trial of Travis McMichael, Gregory McMichael, and William 'Roddie' Bryan for the brutal, racist killing of Ahmaud Arbery. They were appalled by the McMichaels' racist language and deep-seated hatred. How can a heart harbor such hate? Whether in personal relationships or politics, how can people call wrong right and right wrong? How can someone chase and kill a stranger in the street? As Dr. Isaac Singleton said, 'the heart of the problem is the heart problem."

Jer 17:9 NKJV "The heart is deceitful above all things, and desperately wicked, Who can Know it?"

When you think of world history, what is the best thing you've heard/seen a human being doing?

_____

What is the worst thing you've ever heard of human beings doing?

_____

What do you think deceitful means?

_____

Is it possible for one to deceive oneself?

_____

Does this verse help your understanding of man's inhumanity to man?

_____

If it does, what does it tell you about injustice?

_____

THE HUMAN HEART

The depth and heights of the heart of man continue.

Isa 58:2 MSG They're busy, busy, busy at worship, and love studying all about me. To all appearances they're a nation of right-living people— law-abiding, God-honoring. They ask me, 'What's the right thing to do?' and love having me on their side.

Isa 58:3 MSG But they also complain, 'Why do we fast, and you don't look our way? Why do we humble ourselves and you don't even notice?' "Well, here's why: "The bottom line on your 'fast days' is profit. You drive your employees much too hard.

Isa 58:4 MSG You fast, but at the same time you bicker and fight. You fast, but you swing a mean fist. The kind of fasting you do won't get your prayers off the ground.

Isa 58:5 MSG Do you think this is the kind of fast day I'm after: a day to show off humility? To put on a pious long face and parade around solemnly in black. Do you call that fasting, a fast day that I, GOD, would like?

Isa 58:6 MSG This is the kind of fast day I'm after: to break the chains of injustice, get rid of exploitation in the workplace, free the oppressed, cancel debts.

Isa 58:7 MSG What I'm interested in seeing you do is: sharing your food with the hungry, inviting the homeless poor into your homes, putting clothes on the shivering ill-clad, being available to your own families.

Isa 58:8 MSG Do this and the lights will turn on, and your lives will turn around at once. Your righteousness will pave your way. The GOD of glory will secure your passage.

Isa 58:9 MSG Then when you pray, GOD will answer. You'll call out for help, and I'll say, 'Here I am.' "If you get rid of unfair practices, quit blaming victims, quit gossiping about other people's sins,

Isa 58:10 MSG If you are generous with the hungry and start giving yourselves to the down-and-out, your lives will begin to glow in the darkness, your shadowed lives will be bathed in sunlight.

Is it possible for entire religious denominations or (even nations) groups to miss God altogether?

What do these verses tell us about where or how Gods people went wrong?

_____

What did they seem to be doing right?

_____

Why did God reject their worship?

_____

CHAPTER 6

Knowing The Ways of the Unjust

- *Key Point:* How do the actions of the unjust oppress the poor?

- *Discussion Prompt:* What are some ways we can defend the rights of the poor and needy?

- *Possible Answers:*

  Defending the rights of the poor and needy is a crucial aspect of promoting justice and equity in our communities. Here are some ways we can actively work towards this goal:

  From your document:

  1. **Education and Awareness:** *Educate community members about their rights and the importance of justice. Awareness campaigns can help people* understand the significance of justice and how they can contribute to it.

  2. **Community Engagement:** *Encourage active participation in community activities and decision-making processes. When people are involved, they are more likely to advocate for justice and hold authorities accountable.*

  3. **Support for Marginalized Groups:** *Provide support and resources to marginalized and vulnerable groups. This can include legal aid, social services, and economic opportunities to help them overcome systemic barriers.*

  4. **Advocating for Justice:** *Stand up for the oppressed*

and marginalized, ensuring that their voices are heard and their rights are protected. This can include activism, legal advocacy, and community organizing.

By implementing these steps, we can make a significant impact in our communities and help ensure that justice flows like a mighty river.

Job 24:1 NKJV *Since* times are not hidden from the Almighty, why do those who Know Him see not His days?

Job 24:2 NKJV *Some* remove landmarks; They seize flocks violently and feed *on them.*

Job 24:3 NKJV They drive away the donkey of the fatherless; They take the widow's ox as a pledge.

Job 24:4 NKJV They push the needy off the road; All the poor of the land are forced to hide.

Psa 82:3 NKJV Defend the poor and fatherless; Do justice to the afflicted and needy.

Mat 19:21 NKJV Jesus said to him, "If you want to be perfect, go, sell what you have and give to the poor, and you will have treasure in heaven; and come, follow Me."

Jas 2:5 NKJV Listen, my beloved brethren: Has God not chosen the poor of this world *to be* rich in faith and heirs of the kingdom which He promised to those who love Him?

Jas 2:6 NKJV But you have dishonored the poor man. Do not the rich oppress you and drag you into the courts?

Do these passages seem to say that all poverty comes from laziness, or are there other forces that may cause poverty?

_____

What are some of the forces that may cause people to be poor?

_____

Name some ways we can do justice to the afflicted and needy.
(Psalm 82:3)

_____

CHAPTER 7

Knowing God's Justice

- **Key Point:** The differences between biblical justice and human justice.

- **Discussion Prompt:** How can we align our understanding of justice with God's justice?

- **Possible Answers:**

  Aligning our understanding of justice with God's justice involves recognizing and embodying the principles of justice as outlined in the Bible. Here are some key points from your document that can guide us:

  From your document:

  1. **Divine Nature**: Justice is a core attribute of God's character. The Bible often describes God as just and righteous, emphasizing that His actions and judgments are fair and equitable. For example, Deuteronomy 32:4 states, "He is the Rock, his works are perfect, and all his ways are just. A faithful God who does no wrong, upright and just is he".

  2. **Moral Foundation**: The Bible provides a moral framework for human behavior, and justice is a key component of this framework. It calls for fair treatment of all individuals, protection of the vulnerable, and accountability for wrongdoing. This is evident in passages like Micah 6:8, which says, "He has shown you, O mortal, what is good. And what does the Lord require of you? To act justly and to love mercy and to walk humbly with your God".

3. *Social Justice*: The Bible advocates for social justice, urging believers to care for the poor, the oppressed, and the marginalized. This theme is prevalent in the teachings of the prophets and in the ministry of Jesus. For instance, Isaiah 1:17 instructs, "Learn to do right; seek justice. Defend the oppressed. Take up the cause of the fatherless; plead the case of the widow".

By understanding and using these principles, we can work towards creating a just and equitable world that reflects God's character and intentions for humanity.

HOW DO THESE SCRIPTURES ANSWER THE FOLLOWING QUESTIONS?

How does the concept of justice differ between the Old and New Testaments? (Exodus 21:23-25 vs Matthew 5:38-42)

_____

What are some examples of God's justice and mercy in the Bible? (Genesis 18:16-33, Jonah 3-4, Romans 9:14-18)

_____

How does the biblical idea of justice relate to the modern notions of human rights and social justice? (Micah 6:8, Isaiah 58:6-7, James 1:27)

_____

How can Christian's practice justice in their personal and professional lives? (Colossians 3:23-25, Ephesians 4:28, Proverbs 31:8-9)

_____

List four challenges and pitfalls of pursuing justice in a fallen world? (Ecclesiastes 4:1-3, Psalm 73, Habakkuk 1:2-4)

_____

How does the gospel of Jesus Christ reveal God's justice and righteousness? (Romans 3:21-26, 2 Corinthians 5:21, Galatians 3:13-14)

How does the resurrection of Christ affirm God's justice and power over evil? (Acts 17:30-31, Romans 6:5-11, Revelation 20:11-15)

How does the cross of Christ demonstrate both God's love and wrath? (John 3:16, Romans 5:8, Revelation 19:11-16)

How does the Holy Spirit enable and empower Christians to live justly and righteously?
(John 16:8-11, Galatians 5:16-26, Ephesians 5:8-10)

CHAPTER 8

Knowing How to Walk Your Justice

- **Key Point:** *The practical application of biblical justice in our lives.*

- **Discussion Prompt:** *What are some steps we can take to walk in justice daily?*

- **Possible Answers:**

  Walking in justice daily involves integrating principles of fairness, compassion, and integrity into our everyday actions. Here are some practical steps you can take:

  - **Educate Yourself and Others**: *Understanding the root causes and impacts of injustice can help you become a more effective advocate. Educate yourself and others about issues of injustice and the importance of justice.*

  - **Engage with Your Community**: *Participate in local events, join advocacy groups, and support initiatives that promote justice and equality. Active community engagement helps ensure that justice is upheld and authorities are held accountable.*

  - **Support Marginalized Groups**: *Provide support and resources to marginalized and vulnerable groups. This can include offering legal aid, social services, and economic opportunities to help them overcome systemic barriers.*

  - **Act with Compassion and Empathy**: *Treat everyone with the same respect and kindness you desire. Compassion and empathy* *are essential in promoting justice and ensuring fair treatment for all.*

- ○ ***Advocate for Justice****: Stand up for the oppressed and marginalized, ensuring that their voices are heard and their rights are protected. This can include activism, legal advocacy, and community organizing.*

By incorporating these steps into your daily life, you can contribute to creating a more just and equitable world.

Review statements along with supporting paragraphs and scriptures. Ask God to apply important justice principles to areas of your life where you've experienced difficulties.

Biblical justice is based on God's eternal standard of goodness and rightness, rooted in Imago Dei (Gn 1:26). God is the only perfect, eternal, immovable standard for justice (Dt 32:4, Ps 9:1-2). All people are made in God's image, with dignity and immeasurable worth.

Human justice relies on the changing standards of morality and legality in human societies, influenced by culture, history, politics, and personal preferences. It often fails to recognize the inherent value and equality of all people, especially the marginalized and oppressed. **Isaiah 5:20** (NIV): Woe to those who call evil good and good evil, who put darkness for light and light for darkness, who put bitter for sweet and sweet for bitter.

Biblical justice requires freedom, accountability, restoration, and transformation. It focuses not only on punishing wrongdoers but also on restoring victims and reconciling relationships. Aiming to bring God's shalom (peace) to the world, biblical justice is motivated by God's love and grace, empowering people to live according to His will and purpose. **Micah 6:8** (NIV): He has shown you, O mortal, what is good. And what does the Lord require of you? To act justly and to love mercy and to walk humbly with your God

Human justice demands compliance, retribution, compensation, and deterrence. It focuses on enforcing societal laws and rules, imposing penalties on lawbreakers, and restoring the status quo. Driven by human anger and fear, it often creates more resentment and violence. **Romans 13:1-4** (NIV): Let everyone be subject to the governing authorities, for there is no authority except that which God has established. The authorities that exist have been established by God. Consequently, whoever rebels against the authority is rebelling against what God has instituted, and those who do so will bring judgment on themselves. For rulers hold no terror for those who do right, but for those who do wrong. Do you want to be free from fear of the one in authority? Then do what is right and you will be commended. For the one in authority is God's servant for your good. But if you do wrong, be afraid, for rulers do not bear the sword for no reason. They are God's servants, agents of wrath to bring punishment on the wrongdoer

Biblical justice is revealed and fulfilled in Jesus Christ, the perfect embodiment of God's justice. He came to save the world from sin and death, demonstrating God's justice by healing the sick, feeding the hungry, forgiving sinners, and dying on the cross for our sake. Jesus invites us to follow Him and participate in His kingdom of justice and righteousness. **Colossians 1:15-20** (NIV): The Son is the image of the invisible God, the firstborn over all creation. For in him all things were created: things in heaven and on earth, visible and invisible, whether thrones or powers or rulers or authorities; all things have been created through him and for him. He is before all things, and in him all things hold together. And he is the head of the body, the church; he is the beginning and the firstborn from among the dead, so that in everything he might have the supremacy. For God was pleased to have all his fullness dwell in him, and through him to reconcile to himself all things, whether things on earth or things in heaven, by making peace through his blood, shed on the cross.

Human justice is challenged and transformed by Jesus Christ, the ultimate judge who will come again to judge the living and the dead. He exposed the hypocrisy and injustice of the religious and political authorities of his time, calling them to repent and believe. Jesus commands us to love God, love our neighbors as ourselves, and seek first His kingdom and justice. **Acts 17:30-31** (NIV): In the past God overlooked such ignorance, but now he commands all people everywhere to repent. For he has set a day when he will judge the world with justice by the man he has appointed. He has given proof of this to everyone by raising him from the dead."

Now that you have gained a better understanding of the differences between biblical justice and social justice, as well as how God reveals his character in justice and righteousness, read the scriptures below and answer the associated questions:

Read Isaiah 1:23; Amos 2:6,7; Micah 6:8 and Deuteronomy 14:28,29, and answer this question:

What are some examples of God's justice in action in the Old Testament?[3]

Read John 16:16-23; Mattew 16:21-23:24;1 John 3:8, and answer this question: How did Jesus demonstrate God's justice in his life, death and resurrection?[4]

Read Micah 6:8; Isaiah 1:17; Galatians 5:22,23; John 16:13, and answer this question: How does the Holy Spirit empower us to pursue justice in our world today?[5]

Read Isaiah 1:17; Amos 5:24; Micah 6:8; Proverbs 31:8,9, and answer this question: What are some of the injustices that God cares about and wants us to address?[6]

---

[3] Grand Canyon University – Theology Thursday: Justice in the Old Testament
[4] Biblegateway.com
[5] Biblestudytools.com
[6] Lifehopeandtruth.com and biblestudytools.com

Read Romans 3:23; Proverbs 21:2; Proverbs 3:5,6; 1 Corinthians 2:14; James 1:5, and answer this question: How can we discern between God's justice and our own biases or preferences[7]?

Read 1 Corinthians 2:14; James 1:5. Answer this question: How can we balance justice and mercy in our relationships with others?[8]

Read Psalm 122:6; Jeremiah 29:7; 1 Timothy 2:1,2; Isaiah 58:6; Micah 6:8 and answer this question: How can we pray for justice and peace in our communities and nations?[9]

Read articles about Sojourners; Association for More Just Society; and World Vision, and answer this question: How can we partner with other Christians and organizations that are working for justice?

Read scriptures Isaiah 59:14.15; Amos 5:12; Micah 7:2,3; Psalm 82:2,4; Proverbs 21:15 and answer this question: What are some of the challenges or obstacles that we may face when we seek justice[10]?

Read scriptures Joshua 1:9; Psalm 27:1; Isaiah 41:10; 2Timothy 1:7; Philippians 4:13 and answer the following question: How can we overcome fear, apathy or discouragement in our pursuit of justice? [11]

Read scriptures Colossians 3:12; Ephesians 4:32 Micah 6:8; Romans 12:15; Galatians 6:2; 1Peter 3:8, and answer the following question: How can we cultivate a heart of compassion and empathy for those who suffer injustice[12]?

---

[7] Christianity.com
[8] Churchgists.com
[9] Praywithconfidence.com

Know Justice Know Peace

CHAPTER 9

Knowing True Worship

- **Key Point:** The importance of worshiping God in spirit and truth.

- **Discussion Prompt:** How does our understanding of justice influence our worship?

- **Possible Answers:**

  Our understanding of justice deeply influences our worship by aligning our hearts and actions with God's character and teachings. In your document, it is emphasized that true worship requires a heart aligned with God's justice1. This means that worship goes beyond rituals and external actions; it involves a sincere connection with God and adherence to His principles of justice.

  When we understand and practice justice, we reflect God's nature, as justice is a core attribute of His character. This understanding guides us to act fairly, protect the vulnerable, and promote social equity, which are all essential aspects of living out our faith. By embodying these principles, our worship becomes more genuine and pleasing to God, as it is rooted in a commitment to righteousness and justice.

Who are these nameless ashen souls stacked like cordwood on the shelves of wooden Guineamen ships? Who were these bodies lifted from home, transported across mysterious seas, by people unknown, criminal oppressors by human standards, who demanded the captives learn quickly, a foreign language under threat of death? Who are these who soon realized the uncertainty of life and the future, for themselves or their kidnapped children? Would we forget their faces if we never saw them? Would it not be more convenient to forget their anguished cry? In our collective consciousness, it hurts to think of it. Wouldn't it feel better to forget? To forget grief, which lasted so long? Most didn't die quickly; they were anguished, often confused, until death. For two hundred years, some 15-17 million people were uprooted from the freedoms of home. As many as 20% of them died en route to America. Many more were unlisted on ship manifests and records, in attempts to avoid governmental or financial inconvenience; therefore, their numbers were likely undercounted in historical reflections.

The whole world wrestles with the question. An entire culture and world are challenged to come to grips with this awful, uncomfortable, centuries-long event, too easy to track, too close to being a current event. It was indeed brutal.

Slavery ended 160 years ago.... didn't it? It was so sick that our national mentality begs to forget it, to forget them, to cyber past our wicked past. Couldn't they just remain nameless? Couldn't we just move on? There is no real value in discussing it, is there? Our children need not witness the sins of the nation's fathers, must they? The whole messy episode is forgettable, isn't it? The USA was a nation warned of its awful slaving and its greedy motives. No less a light than Charles Haddon Spurgeon, the most influential and powerful preacher of the 1800s, told of the sin of American slavery. He was rewarded with book burnings of his writings across the American South and threats to his life. On February 17, 1860, citizens from Montgomery, Alabama, gathered in the jail yard to burn the "dangerous books" of Charles Haddon Spurgeon, the most popular Christian preacher in the Victorian world. A newspaper recorded the event:

"Last Saturday, we devoted to the flames a large number of copies of Spurgeon's Sermons…We trust that the works of the **greasy cockney vociferator** may receive the same treatment throughout the South. And if the Pharisaical author should ever show himself in these parts, we trust that a stout cord may speedily find its way around his eloquent throat." A friend of Frederick Douglas, the London Pastor joined a growing chorus of abolitionist but found a deeply seated hatred, anger and threats in America. Now, Spurgeon is widely quoted in American pulpits while Americans fight to forget the enslaved, he vouched for their freedom."[13] [14]

CHAPTER 10

Knowing The Way to Worship God

- **Key Point:** *The connection between justice and worship.*

- **Discussion Prompt:** *Why does God care about how we do justice before we worship Him?*

- **Possible Answers:**

  God cares about how we do justice before we worship Him because true worship requires a heart aligned with God's justice. This means that worship goes beyond rituals and external actions; it involves a sincere connection with God and adherence to His principles of justice. When we understand and practice justice, we reflect God's nature, as justice is a core attribute of His character. This understanding guides us to act fairly, protect the vulnerable, and promote social equity, which are all essential aspects of living out our faith. By embodying these principles, our worship becomes more genuine and pleasing to God, as it is rooted in a commitment to righteousness and justice.

God is Spirit, and those who worship Him must worship in spirit and truth."0John 4:24 (NKJV)

Read John 4:24. Is any kind of worship acceptable to God?

_____

What do you think Jesus meant when He gave the two ways that true worshippers would worship Him?

_____

Read Isaiah 58:2-6. Why do you think God cares about how we do justice "before" we worship Him?

_____

What might these words from Jesus have to do with it?

_____

Is it surprising to you that God cares so much about justice that He seems to interrupt their worship to demand it?

_____

Read verses 8-11 of this chapter, then list at least 5 things God promises to doers of justice.

{1}_____

{2}_____

{3}_____

{4}_____

{5}_____

Are there personal, spiritual benefits to doing justice?

_____

What are those benefits?

_____

In what ways might your life be better under those benefits?

_____

CHAPTER 11

Knowing How to Impress God

- **Key Point:** *True worship requires a heart aligned with God's justice.*

- **Discussion Prompt:** *What does it mean to worship God in spirit and truth?*

Possible Answers:

To worship God in spirit and truth means to engage in worship that is both sincere and aligned with God's nature and teachings. This concept is rooted in the idea that true worship goes beyond mere rituals and external actions; it involves a heartfelt connection with God and adherence to His truth.

Matt 15:8 NKJV "These people draw near to me with their mouth, and honor me with their lips, but their heart is far from me.

Matt 15:9 NKJV And in vain they worship me, teaching as doctrines the commandments of men."

Jesus, here, is apparently not impressed even when one's words are right. He's not even satisfied when He's honored. Even worship can be "in vain".

What does Jesus seem to say is required to truly draw near Him?

_____

Pro 17:16 NKJV "Why *is there* in the hand of a fool the purchase price of wisdom, since *he has* no heart *for it?* "

What is the price of wisdom?

_____

Psalms 12:2 NKJV "They speak idly everyone with his neighbor; *With* flattering lips *and* a double heart they speak. "

What do these verses have in common with Matt. 15:8,9 when describing the origin of sin?

_____

Matt 5:8 NKJV "Blessed *are* the pure in heart, for they shall see God. "

What is promised here, for the "pure in heart"?

_____

Rom 2:5 NKJV But in accordance with your hardness and your impenitent heart you are treasuring up for yourself wrath in the day of wrath and revelation of the righteous judgment of God, …

What does this verse promise for the wicked hearted person?

_____

CHAPTER 12

Knowing The Price of Pride

- **Key Point:** *The dangers of pride and its impact on justice.*

- **Discussion Prompt:** *How can we avoid the pride that leads to injustice?*

- **Possible Answers***:*

  Avoiding the pride that leads to injustice is crucial for maintaining fairness and integrity in leadership. Here are some strategies to help prevent pride from influencing decisions and actions:

  1. **Cultivate Humility***: Leaders should practice humility by acknowledging their limitations and being open to learning from others. This involves recognizing that they do not have all the answers and valuing the contributions of their team members.*

  2. **Seek Diverse Perspectives***: By actively seeking out and considering diverse viewpoints, leaders can avoid the narrow-mindedness that often accompanies pride. This helps in making more balanced and just decisions.*

  3. **Encourage Feedback***: Creating an environment where feedback is welcomed and valued can help leaders stay grounded. Constructive criticism from peers and subordinates can provide valuable insights and prevent leaders from becoming overly self-assured.*

4. **Reflect on Actions and Decisions**: Regular self-reflection enables leaders to critically assess their actions and decisions. This practice helps in identifying any biases or prideful tendencies that may have influenced their behavior.

5. **Prioritize the Greater Good**: Leaders should focus on the well-being of their team and organization, rather than their personal interests or ego. Making decisions that benefit the collective rather than serving personal interests can help mitigate the effects of pride.

6. **Stay Accountable**: Establishing accountability mechanisms, such as advisory boards or peer reviews, can help leaders remain answerable for their actions. This external oversight can act as a check against prideful behavior.

By integrating these practices into their leadership approach, leaders can foster an environment of justice and righteousness, free from the detrimental effects of pride.

"I never thought in my lifetime I would see Richmond and Charlottesville get rid of their statues. They're idols of white supremacy and symbols of racism and hate. And for me, as a Christian, and many other faiths feel this way too, we can't have idols in our public square. That just doesn't square right with what we're trying to do as a community, as a state, a commonwealth, or a nation."

~ Robert W. Lee, descendant of Confederate General Robert E. Lee, author, "A Sin By Any Other Name" [15]

Hos 13:6 NKJV "When they had pasture, they were filled; They were filled, and their heart was exalted; Therefore, they forgot Me."

---

[15] Robert W. Lee, descendant of Confederate General Robert E. Lee, author, "A Sin By Any Other Name." NPR Interview on April 2, 2019.

Let us look at this verse from a more modern translation, then answer the question.

Here is the Good News translation: "Hos.13:6"But when you entered the good land, you became full and satisfied, and then you grew proud and forgot me."

What do you think caused them to forget God?

_____

How can one avoid the pride of heart that leads to separation from God?

_____

Read James 2:1-9 GNT

"1 My friends, as believers in our Lord Jesus Christ, the Lord of glory, you must never treat people in different ways according to their outward appearance. 2 Suppose a rich man wearing gold ring and fine clothes comes to your meeting, and a poor man in ragged clothes also comes. 3 If you show more respect to the well-dressed man and say to him, "Have this best seat here," but say to the poor man, "Stand over there, or sit here on the floor by my feet," 4 then you are guilty of creating distinctions among yourselves and of making judgments based on evil motives.

5 Listen, my dear friends! God chose the poor people of this world to be rich in faith and to possess the kingdom which he promised to those who love him. 6 But you dishonor the poor! Who are the ones who oppress you and drag you before the judges? The rich! 7 They are the ones who speak evil of that good name which has been given to you.

8 You will be doing the right thing if you obey the law of the Kingdom, which is found in the scripture, "Love your neighbor as you love yourself." 9 But if you treat people according to their outward appearance, you are guilty of sin, and the Law condemns you as a lawbreaker."

- Some were trained to dislike or treat people unfairly or discriminate?

- Some were trained to believe that "others" should be treated as less than oneself?

- How can one change their heart if those they have loved and respected taught them differently from what God's Word teaches?

- What can one do if this is what they have learned?

Mat 5:8 NKJV "Blessed *are* the pure in heart, for they shall see God. " Can a rich or proud man be pure in heart?

CHAPTER 13

Knowing My Pain

- **Key Point:** *The cry for justice from those who have been wronged.*

- **Discussion Prompt:** *Why is it important for God to avenge the blood of the innocent?*

- **Possible answers:**

  1. *In Revelation 6:10, the martyrs cry out to God, asking, "How long, Sovereign Lord, holy and true, until you judge the inhabitants of the earth and avenge our blood?" This verse highlights the deep desire for justice and the importance of God avenging the blood of the innocent.*

  2. *From your document, it is emphasized that the cry for justice from those who have been wronged*

is significant because it reflects God's character and His commitment to justice1. God's avenging of the innocent's blood is crucial for several reasons:

- **Divine Justice**: *It upholds the principle that God is just and righteous. By avenging the blood of the innocent, God demonstrates His commitment to justice and righteousness, ensuring that evil and wrongdoing do not go unpunished.*

- **Moral Order**: *It maintains the moral order of the universe. When innocent blood is shed, it disrupts the moral fabric of society. God's intervention restores* *balance and order, affirming that justice will prevail.*

■ ***Deterrence of Evil****: It acts as a deterrent to evil. Knowing that God will avenge the innocent can discourage individuals from committing acts of violence and injustice, promoting a more just and peaceful society.*

Rev.6:9 NKJV When He opened the fifth seal, I saw under the altar the souls of those who had been slain for the word of God and for the testimony which they held.

Rev 6:10 NKJV And they cried with a loud voice, saying, «How long, O Lord, holy and true, until You judge and avenge our blood on those who dwell on the earth?»

Rev 6:11 NKJV Then a white robe was given to each of them; and it was said to them that they should rest a little while longer, until both *the number of* their fellow servants and their brethren, who would be killed as they *were,* was completed.

- Wouldn't you think that when you finally get to Heaven that nothing else matters?

- Wouldn't it seem that once arriving at Gods throne, that you wouldn't care what others did to you on earth?

- Why would you think these believers were "crying "out to God to avenge their blood and take revenge on their murderers?

_____

Which of these reasons would explain why God, in Heaven, said He would avenge them?

God is the God of Justice _____
(Yes or No)

God wanted them to stop their protest

_____

So, they could get out from under the throne?

_____

God has to balance the scales of Justice even in eternity

_____

CHAPTER 14

Knowing The Injustice of Man

1. **Key Point:** *The consequences of being neutral in situations of injustice.*

2. **Discussion Prompt:** *How can we actively stand against injustice in our daily lives?*

3. **Possible Answers:**

4. *Standing against injustice in our daily lives involves several practical steps that align with biblical principles. Here are some ways to actively oppose injustice:*

   ○ **Education and Awareness:** *Educate yourself and others about the issues of injustice. Understanding the root causes and impacts of injustice can help you become a more effective advocate.*

   ○ **Community Engagement:** *Get involved in your community. Participate in local events, join advocacy groups, and support initiatives that promote justice and equality.*

   ○ **Support for Marginalized Groups:** *Provide support to marginalized and vulnerable groups. This can include offering legal aid, social services, and economic opportunities to help them overcome systemic barriers.*

   ○ **Compassion and Empathy:** *Act with compassion and empathy towards others. Treat everyone with the same respect and kindness you desire.*

"If you are neutral in situations of injustice, you have chosen the side of the oppressor."
— Desmond Tutu

Judges 6:3 NKJV So it was, whenever Israel had sown, Midianites would come up; also, Amalekites and the people of the East would come up against them.

Judges 6:4 NKJV Then they would encamp against them and destroy the produce of the earth as far as Gaza, and leave no sustenance for Israel, neither sheep nor ox nor donkey.

Judges 6:5 NKJV For they would come up with their livestock and their tents, coming in as numerous as locusts; both they and their camels were without number; and they would enter the land to destroy it.

Judges 6:6 NKJV So Israel was greatly impoverished because of the Midianites, and the children of Israel cried out to the LORD.

Judges 6:7 NKJV And it came to pass, when the children of Israel cried out to the LORD because of the Midianites,

Judges 6:8 NKJV that the LORD sent a prophet to the children of Israel, who said to them, "Thus says the LORD God of Israel: 'I brought you up from Egypt and brought you out of the house of bondage.

Was Gideon the Prophet in verse 8?

_____

If not, then who?

_____

Judges 6:9 NKJV and I delivered you out of the hand of the Egyptians and out of the hand of all who oppressed you, and drove them out before you and gave you, their land.

Was the poverty of Israel caused by their laziness?

_____

Why do you think these enemies would ruin the works of Gods people?

_____

Could such a thing happen Today?

_____

In what ways might that be happening in the 21st century?

_____

Jer 17:9 NKJV «The heart *is* deceitful above all *things,* and desperately wicked; Who can Know it? Does this verse help your understanding of man's inhumanity to man?

_____

If it does, what does it tell you about injustice?

_____

CHAPTER 15

Knowing Injustice

- **Key Point:** *The various forms of injustice in the world and how they differ from biblical justice.*

- **Discussion Prompt:** *How can we practice biblical justice in a world filled with injustice?*

- **Possible Answers:**

  Practicing biblical justice in a world filled with injustice involves aligning our actions with the principles of justice as outlined in the Bible. Here are some key points from your document that can guide us:

  From your document:

  1. **Understanding God's Heart for Justice***: Recognize that justice is a core attribute of God's character. The Bible describes God as just and righteous, emphasizing that His*

  actions and judgments are fair and equitable. For example, Deuteronomy 32:4 states, "He is the Rock, his works are perfect, and all his ways are just. A faithful God who does no wrong, upright and just is he".

  2. **Moral Foundation***: The Bible provides a moral framework for human behavior, calling for fair treatment of all individuals, protection of the vulnerable, and accountability for wrongdoing. Micah 6:8 says, "He has shown you, O mortal, what is good. And what does the Lord require of you? To act justly and to love mercy and to walk humbly with your God".*

3. *Social Justice*: *The Bible advocates for social justice, urging believers to care for the poor, the oppressed, and the marginalized. Isaiah 1:17 instructs, "Learn to do right; seek justice. Defend the oppressed. Take up the cause of the fatherless; plead the case of the widow".*

4. *Practical Steps*: *To practice biblical justice, we can:*

   - *Educate and Raise Awareness*: *Educate community members about their rights and the importance of justice. Awareness campaigns can help people understand the significance of justice and how they can contribute to it.*

   - *Engage with the Community*: *Encourage active participation in community activities and decision-making processes. When people are involved, they are more likely to advocate for justice and hold authorities accountable.*

   - *Support Marginalized Groups*: *Provide support and resources to marginalized and vulnerable groups. This can include legal aid, social services, and economic opportunities to help them overcome systemic barriers.*

By understanding and applying these principles, we can strive to create a just and equitable world that reflects God's character and intentions for humanity.

Injustice in the world refers to a lack of fairness, manifesting as social, economic, political, legal, and environmental injustices.

Is injustice in the world the same as injustice in the Bible?

_____

Biblically, how do we NOT become practitioners of injustice?

_____

Lev 19:15 NKJV ‹You shall do no injustice in judgment. You shall not be partial to the poor, nor honor the person of the mighty. In righteousness you shall judge your neighbor.

In making a judgement who shall we give honor to?

  a. A poor friend that we Know is an honorable person.
  b. A rich man who has offered me my perfect job..
  c. My brother just won the lottery.
  d. A homeless mother who needs to get off the streets.
  e. None of the above

Why might the verse specifically mention not being partial to the poor or deferring to the great?

_____

What does the verse instruct about showing partiality in judgment?

_____

Zep 3:5 ESV The LORD within her is righteous; he does no injustice; every morning he shows forth his justice; each dawn he does not fail; but the unjust Knows no shame.

Who is "her" in Zep 3:5?

  a. God
  b. Jerusalem
  c. Judah
  d. Ninevah

Rom 9:14 ESV What shall we say then? Is there injustice on God›s part? By no means!

If we have undeniable evidence that God has injustice, how do we solve that problem?

_____

CHAPTER 16

Knowing What To Do

- **Key Point:** *The call to serve the least of these as a way to serve Jesus.*

- **Discussion Prompt:** *How can we practically serve the marginalized in our communities?*

- **Possible Answers:**

  Serving the marginalized in our communities is a vital aspect of fostering justice and equity. Here are some practical ways to make a meaningful impact:

  1. **Volunteer Your Time**: *Engage with local organizations that support marginalized groups. This could include shelters, food banks, community centers, or advocacy groups. Your time and skills can make a significant difference.*

  2. **Provide Financial Support**: *Donate to organizations that work directly with marginalized communities. Even small contributions can help fund essential services and programs.*

  3. **Advocate for Change**: *Use your voice to advocate for policies and practices that promote equity and justice. This can involve writing to local representatives, participating in community meetings, or supporting campaigns that address systemic issues.*

  4. **Offer Professional Services**: *If you have specialized skills, consider offering them pro bono to those in need. This could*

include legal advice, medical care, educational tutoring, or career counseling.

5. **Create Inclusive Spaces**: Ensure that your workplace, community groups, and social circles are inclusive and welcoming to all. This involves actively challenging discrimination and promoting diversity.

6. **Educate Yourself and Others**: Learn about the challenges faced by marginalized communities and share this knowledge with others. Understanding the root causes of inequality can help you become a more effective advocate and ally.

7. **Support Local Businesses**: Patronize businesses owned by marginalized individuals. This helps to economically empower these communities and promote their growth and sustainability.

8. **Build Relationships**: Take the time to build genuine relationships with individuals from marginalized communities. Listening to their experiences and understanding their needs can guide your efforts to support them effectively.

By integrating these actions into your daily life, you can contribute to a more just and equitable society.

...KNOWING THE LEAST OF THESE...

Mat 25:35 NKJV for I was hungry, and you gave Me food; I was thirsty, and you gave Me drink; I was a stranger and you took Me in;

Mat 25:36 NKJV I *was* naked, and you clothed Me; I was sick, and you visited Me; I was in prison, and you came to Me.'

What do the classes of people listed by Jesus have in common?

_____

What are the traditional ways that you may Know or have heard about to address each of these groups named?

_____

"Ah! poor negro slave, every scar upon your back shall have a stripe of honor in heaven."
Charles Haddon Spurgeon

In Matthew 25:35, Jesus made the needy and poor Himself, in that verse. What does that say about God's heart for the destitute and abused?

_____

What would this verse seem to say is the best way to get to Jesus?

_____

"Justice will not be served until those who are unaffected are as outraged as those who are."
Benjamin Franklin

CHAPTER 17

Knowing Outrage

- **Key Point:** *The need for justice to be plentiful and the role of outrage in serving justice.*

- **Discussion Prompt:** *How can we channel our outrage into positive actions for justice?*

- **Possible Answers:**

  Serving the marginalized in our communities is a vital aspect of promoting justice and equity. Here are some practical ways to do so:

  ### From your document:

  1. **Education and Awareness:** *Educate community members about their rights and the importance of justice. Awareness campaigns can help people understand the significance of justice and how they can contribute to it.*

2. **Community Engagement:** *Encourage active participation in community activities and decision-making processes. When people are involved, they are more likely to advocate for justice and hold authorities accountable.*

3. **Support for Marginalized Groups:** *Provide support and resources to marginalized and vulnerable groups. This can include legal aid, social services, and economic opportunities to help them overcome systemic barriers.*

4. **Compassion and Empathy:** *Act with compassion and empathy towards others. Treat everyone with the same respect and kindness you desire.*

5. Advocating for Justice: *Stand up for the oppressed and marginalized, ensuring that their voices are heard and their rights are protected. This can include activism, legal advocacy, and community organizing.*

By implementing these steps, we can make a significant impact in our communities and help ensure that justice flows like a mighty river.

Psalms 82:3 NKJV Defend the poor and fatherless; Do justice to the afflicted and needy.

In this verse the word ..."justice" is tsâdaq (tsaw dak). This word often means, "to make right". Sometimes it's translated, "to cleanse". When you think of the need for justice in your city or country, how does either meaning affect what you are seeing?

_____

Do you believe you can commit your life to justice?

_____

List at least three ways you can obey this verse.

_____

Can we be outraged and still serve justice when injustice is being served and harbored by the people in power. Paul and Silas were arrested, dragged, tied up, stripped, beaten with rods, chained, feet put in stocks, and unfairly accused because of also being Jewish.

_____

Can Paul and Silas be defended from this type of injustice?

_____

What steps should someone who receives injustice like Paul and Silas take to be healed of this type of injustice?

_____

CHAPTER 18

Knowing The Plan of God

- **Key Point:** The gospel message and its implications for justice.

- **Discussion Prompt:** How does the gospel guide our pursuit of justice?

- **Possible Answers:**

  The gospel provides a profound foundation for our pursuit of justice by aligning our actions with God's character and teachings. It emphasizes that justice is a core attribute of God's nature, and as believers, we are called to reflect this in our lives. Here are some key points from your document that highlight how the gospel guides our pursuit of justice:

  1. **Understanding God's Heart for Justice**: The Bible describes God as just and righteous, emphasizing that His actions and judgments are fair and equitable. For example, Deuteronomy 32:4 states, "He is the Rock, his works are perfect, and all his ways are just. A faithful God who does no wrong, upright and just is he".

  2. **Moral Foundation**: The Bible provides a moral framework for human behavior, calling for fair treatment of all individuals, protection of the vulnerable, and accountability for wrongdoing. Micah 6:8 says, "He has shown you, O mortal, what is good. And what does the Lord require of you? To act justly and to love mercy and to walk humbly with your God".

3. _Social Justice_: _The Bible advocates for social justice, urging believers to care for the poor, the oppressed, and the marginalized. Isaiah 1:17 instructs, "Learn to do right; seek justice. Defend the oppressed. Take up the cause of the fatherless; plead the case of the widow"._

By understanding and using these principles, we can work towards creating a just and equitable world that reflects God's character and intentions for humanity.

Gal 2:7 MSG It was soon evident that God had entrusted me with the same message to the non-Jews as Peter had been preaching to the Jews.

Gal 2:9 MSG Recognizing that my calling had been given by God, James, Peter, and John—the pillars of the church—shook hands with me and Barnabas, assigning us to a ministry to the non-Jews, while they continued to be responsible for reaching out to the Jews.

Gal 2:10 MSG The only additional thing they asked was that we remember the poor, and I was already eager to do that.

Many translations refer to this message, entrusted by God to Paul, as "the gospel." Read these two passages, then name at least 4 (or 5) things that make the gospel actually "the gospel"?

(1 Cor. 15: 1-6: Gal. 4:1-6)

[1]_____

[2]_____

[3]_____

[4]_____

[5]_____

Why do you suppose God assigned Peter and Paul to reach out to two diverse kinds of people with the same message?

_____

Do you have an opinion about how this message may have been structured to reach "non-Jews"?

_____

Though the key leaders approved the message of Paul, what was the one thing they insisted must be included?

_____

Do you understand why such an ordinary thing as poverty would be so important to God?

_____

How should a church respond to poverty?

_____

How can an individual respond to or help the poor?

_____

CHAPTER 19

Knowing Biblical Justice in Society

- **Key Point:** *The relationship between biblical justice and societal justice.*

- **Discussion Prompt:** *How can we influence society with biblical principles of justice?*

- **Possible Answers:**

  Influencing society with biblical principles of justice involves understanding and embodying the core attributes of God's character as outlined in the Bible. Here are some key points from your document that can guide us:

  From your document

  1. **Divine Nature**: *Justice is a core attribute of God's character. The Bible often describes God as just and righteous, emphasizing that His actions and judgments are fair and equitable. For example,* Deuteronomy 32:4 *states, "He is the Rock, his works are perfect, and all his ways are just. A faithful God who does no wrong, upright and just is he".*

  2. **Moral Foundation**: *The Bible provides a moral framework for human behavior, and justice is a key component of this framework. It calls for fair treatment of all individuals, protection of the vulnerable, and accountability for wrongdoing. This is evident in passages like Micah 6:8, which states, "He has shown you, O mortal, what is good. And what does the Lord require of you? To act justly and to love mercy and to walk humbly with your God."*

3. **Social Justice**: The Bible advocates for social justice, urging believers to care for the poor, the oppressed, and the marginalized. This theme is prevalent in the teachings of the prophets and in the ministry of Jesus. For instance, Isaiah 1:17 instructs, "Learn to do right; seek justice. Defend the oppressed. Take up the cause of the fatherless; plead the case of the widow".

4. **Practical Steps**: To practice biblical justice, we can:

   - **Educate and Raise Awareness**: Educate community members about their rights and the importance of justice. Awareness campaigns can help people understand the significance of justice and how they can contribute to it.

   - **Engage with the Community**: Encourage active participation in community activities and decision-making processes. When people are involved, they are more likely to advocate for justice and hold authorities accountable.

   - **Support Marginalized Groups**: Provide support and resources to marginalized and vulnerable groups. This can include legal aid, social services, and economic opportunities to help them overcome systemic barriers.

By understanding and using these principles, we can work towards creating a just and equitable world that reflects God's character and intentions for humanity.

Are our Christian standards the same as the world's? Can we be good citizens yet miss the mark with God? The Pharisees, religious leaders in the New Testament, were known for their strict observance of Jewish laws. Yet, Jesus criticized them for neglecting the more important aspects of the law: 'justice, mercy, and faithfulness' (Matthew 23:23, ESV). This suggests that even those who are externally righteous and perform good deeds can miss the heart of what God desires. While philanthropy and good deeds align with biblical principles, Christian teachings emphasize the importance of a personal relationship with God, repentance, and faith in Jesus Christ. Good works alone, without faith and a right heart towards God, might be seen as missing the mark in Christian theology.

How does the biblical instruction of "loving your neighbor" influence our society's understanding of justice? (Mark 12:31)

_____

In what ways does today's justice system mirror the biblical principle of impartiality in judgment? (Leviticus 19:15)

_____

How does the societal shift towards restorative justice align with the teachings of reconciliation in the Bible? (2 Corinthians 5:18-19)

_____

How does our society protect the rights of the marginalized compared to biblical exhortations? (Psalm 82:3)

_____

How do modern labor laws reflect the biblical teachings about fair wages? (James 5:4)

_____

In what ways does the Bible's emphasis on truth-seeking challenge our justice system? (Proverbs 12:17)

_____

CHAPTER 20

Knowing Biblical Justice and the Laws

- **Key Point:** The biblical commands to defend the rights of the poor and needy.

- **Discussion Prompt:** How do our societal laws reflect or differ from biblical justice?

- **Possible Answers:**

  The comparison between societal laws and biblical justice can be quite insightful. Let's explore this topic based on the information from your document.

- **From your document:**

  ○ Biblical justice is deeply rooted in the character of God and is a core attribute of His nature. The Bible describes God as just and righteous, emphasizing that His actions and judgments are fair and equitable. For example,

Deuteronomy 32:4 states, "He is the Rock, his works are perfect, and all his ways are just. A faithful God who does no wrong, upright and just is he". This divine nature of justice calls for fair treatment of all individuals, protection of the vulnerable, and accountability for wrongdoing.

  ○ In contrast, societal laws are created by human institutions and can vary widely depending on cultural, political, and historical contexts. While many societal laws aim to promote justice and fairness, they may not always align perfectly with the principles of biblical justice. For instance, *societal laws might focus more on legal procedures and regulations, whereas biblical justice emphasizes moral and ethical conduct, compassion, and social equity.*

○ *One key difference is that biblical justice advocates for social justice, urging believers to care for the poor, the oppressed, and the marginalized. This theme is prevalent in the teachings of the prophets and in the ministry of Jesus. For example, Isaiah 1:17 instructs, "Learn to do right; seek justice. Defend the oppressed. Take up the cause of the fatherless; plead the case of the widow". Societal laws, on the other hand, may not always prioritize the needs of the marginalized to the same extent.*

The prophets, particularly in the Old Testament, frequently spoke against the rich oppressing the poor or denying them justice (e.g., Amos 5:11-12). Dishonesty using false measures, deceit in trade, or bribery is condemned (e.g., Deuteronomy 25:13-16). Showing favoritism or partiality, especially in judgment, is considered unjust (e.g., Leviticus 19:15). Taking advantage of the vulnerable or using exploitation: such as widows, orphans, and foreigners, is repeatedly condemned (e.g., Zechariah 7:10). Committing acts of violence such as rape, robbery, kidnapping, aggravated assault, battery, slavery or shedding innocent blood is seen as an abomination (e.g., Proverbs 6:16-19).

How does the biblical command to defend the rights of the poor and needy manifest in our society's welfare systems? (Proverbs 31:8-9)

How does our society's understanding of environmental justice mirror biblical stewardship of the earth? (Genesis 2:15)

Do modern concepts of community responsibility align with the biblical idea of bearing one another's burdens? (Galatians 6:2)

_____

In what ways does our society's penal system reflect the biblical principle of "an eye for an eye"? (Exodus 21:24)

_____

How do modern social movements advocating for the oppressed reflect biblical calls for justice? (Isaiah 1:17)

_____

How do our societal views on debt relief relate to biblical practices like the Year of Jubilee? (Leviticus 25:10)

_____

CHAPTER 21

Knowing God's Answer to Discrimination

- **Key Point:** *The Bible's stance on partiality and discrimination.*

- **Discussion Prompt:** *How can we address discrimination within our communities?*

  Possible Answers:

  Addressing discrimination within our communities is a crucial step towards creating a just and equitable society. Here are some key strategies to consider:

  From your document:

  1. **Education and Awareness**: *Educate community members about their rights and the importance of justice. Awareness campaigns can help people understand the*

  significance of justice and how they can contribute to it.

  2. **Community Engagement**: *Encourage active participation in community activities and decision-making processes. When people are involved, they are more likely to advocate for justice and hold authorities accountable.*

  3. **Support for Marginalized Groups**: *Provide support and resources to marginalized and vulnerable groups. This can include legal aid, social services, and economic opportunities to help them overcome systemic barriers.*

4. Compassion and Empathy: *Act with compassion and empathy towards others. Treat everyone with the same respect and kindness you desire.*

5. Advocating for Justice: *Stand up for the oppressed and marginalized, ensuring that their voices are heard and their rights are protected. This can include activism, legal advocacy, and community organizing.*

By implementing these steps, we can make a significant impact in our communities and help ensure that justice flows like a mighty river. How do you think these strategies could be applied in your community?

Many religious individuals and groups recognize racial injustice as a violation of God's principle that all humans are created in His image and are of equal worth and dignity. To obey God's justice, they advocate for racial equality, participate in peaceful protests, and educate others about racial issues. Non-governmental organizations (NGOs) have created or collaborated on programs to support communities disproportionately affected by racial discrimination, providing educational resources, financial support, and safe spaces for dialogue. Consequently, many individuals examine their own biases, seek spiritual guidance to overcome them, and listen to those who have experienced racial discrimination, aiming to be allies and promote justice in their communities.

What does the Bible say about showing partiality based on wealth or social status? (James 2:1-4 (ESV)

_____

What does the Old Testament teach about treating foreigners? (Leviticus 19:34 (ESV)

_____

How does the Bible emphasize that all humans have equal value in the eyes of God? (Genesis 1:27 (ESV)

_____

What does the New Testament teach about the unity of all believers, regardless of race or social status? (Galatians 3:28 (ESV)

_____

What does the Bible say about justice and defending the rights of the marginalized? (Proverbs 31:8-9 (ESV)

_____

How did Jesus challenge societal discrimination during His ministry? (John 4:9 (ESV)

_____

How does the Bible address discrimination within the church community? (1 Corinthians 12:12-13 (ESV)

_____

Know How to Love Mercy

- **Key Point:**

  One of the key points in Chapter 22 is the importance of justice and righteousness in leadership. The chapter emphasizes that true leadership involves not only guiding and directing but also ensuring fairness, equity, and moral integrity in all actions and decisions. This is rooted in the belief that leaders should reflect the character of God, who is just and righteous.

- **Discussion Prompt**

  Discussion Prompt: How can leaders today ensure that their actions and decisions reflect justice and righteousness, especially in challenging and complex situations?

- **Possible Answers:**

  Leaders today can ensure that their actions and decisions reflect justice and righteousness by adopting several key practices:

  1. **Commit to Ethical Standards**: Leaders should establish and adhere to a clear set of ethical guidelines that prioritize fairness, equity, and integrity. This commitment helps in making decisions that are just and morally sound.

  2. **Foster an Inclusive Environment**: By promoting diversity and inclusion, leaders can ensure that different perspectives are considered, leading to more equitable and just outcomes. This involves

actively listening to and valuing the input of all team members.

3. **Transparent Decision-Making:** Transparency in the decision-making process builds trust and accountability. Leaders should communicate the rationale behind their decisions and be open to feedback and scrutiny.

4. **Continuous Learning and Adaptation:** Leaders should stay informed about social justice issues and be willing to adapt their strategies to address new challenges. This includes seeking out training and education on topics related to justice and equity.

5. **Lead by Example:** Demonstrating justice and righteousness in their own behavior sets a powerful example for others to follow. Leaders should model the values they wish to see in their organization.

6. **Engage in Reflective Practices:** Regular self-reflection and seeking feedback from others can help leaders identify areas where they may need to improve in terms of justice and righteousness.

By integrating these practices into their leadership approach, leaders can navigate complex situations while upholding the principles of justice and righteousness.

In the Bible, equity means treating individuals fairly, considering their unique circumstances. Righteousness involves living according to God's laws and is intrinsic to God's nature. Justice emphasizes fair judgment and protecting the vulnerable. While the Bible doesn't use the term 'crisis response,' leaders and prophets often acted in the face of challenges, like Joseph during the famine in Egypt (Genesis 41). Although equity, righteousness, justice, and crisis response can intersect, especially in ethics and morality, they are distinct concepts with unique implications

How does God respond to the prayers of the righteous during crises? (Proverbs 15:29 (ESV)

_____

How are righteousness and equity related in Proverbs?
(Proverbs 21:5 (ESV)

_____

What are the implications of injustice on a society?
(Proverbs 21:15 (ESV)

_____

What does the Bible say about equal treatment in the community?
(Leviticus 24:22 (ESV)

_____

How should we respond when we see someone in crisis?
(Galatians 6:2 (ESV)

_____

How are we to act justly and love mercy? (Micah 6:8 (ESV)

_____

CHAPTER 23

Knowing Justice in Society

- **Key Point:** *The impact of justice on society and the role of Christians.*

- **Discussion Prompt:** *How can we influence society with biblical principles of justice?*

- **Possible Answers:**

  Influencing society with biblical principles of justice involves understanding and embodying the core attributes of God's character as outlined in the Bible. Here are some key points from your document that can guide us:

- **From your document:**

  1. **Divine Nature**: *Justice is a core attribute of God's character. The Bible often describes God as just and righteous, emphasizing that His actions and judgments are fair and equitable. For example, Deuteronomy 32:4 states, "He is the Rock, his works are perfect, and all his ways are just. A faithful God who does no wrong, upright and just is he".*

  2. **Moral Foundation**: *The Bible offers a moral framework for human behavior, with justice being a key component of this framework. It calls for fair treatment of all individuals, protection of the vulnerable, and accountability for wrongdoing. This is evident in passages like Micah 6:8, which says, "He has shown you, O mortal, what is good. And what does the Lord*

require of you? To act justly and to love mercy and to walk humbly with your God".

3. **Social Justice***: The Bible advocates for social justice, urging believers to care for the poor, the oppressed, and the marginalized. This theme is prevalent in the teachings of the prophets and in the ministry of Jesus. For instance, Isaiah 1:17 instructs, "Learn to do right; seek justice. Defend the oppressed. Take up the cause of the fatherless; plead the case of the widow".*

By understanding and applying these principles, we can strive to create a just and equitable world that reflects God's character and intentions for humanity. This involves promoting fairness, protecting the vulnerable, and ensuring accountability for wrongdoing.

Social Injustice: This relates to discrimination or prejudice based on race, gender, age, economic status, religion, nationality, or other societal constructs. It results in certain groups being marginalized, oppressed, or denied basic rights and opportunities.

Economic Injustice: This form of injustice is seen when resources and wealth are unevenly distributed, often due to systems that favor a particular class or group at the expense of others.

Political Injustice: When those in power use their position to benefit themselves or a particular group disproportionately, often suppressing opposition or the rights of minorities.

Legal Injustice: This occurs when laws are applied unevenly or are biased against certain groups, or when the judicial system fails to uphold the rights of individuals.

Environmental Injustice: This can be observed when certain communities face disproportionate exposure to pollutants or environmental hazards, often because they lack the economic or political power to advocate for themselves.

How does societal justice differ from biblical justice? (Micah 6:8)

_____

What role does mercy play in biblical justice compared to societal justice? (Matthew 5:7)

_____

In what ways does society reward or punish just behavior? How does the Bible view rewards for justice? (Matthew 25:34-40)

_____

How does the Bible define justice for the marginalized? How does society approach it? (Psalm 82:3)

_____

How do societal laws on retribution compare with the "eye for an eye" principle in the Old Testament? (Leviticus 24:20)

_____

How does society view forgiveness in justice systems versus biblical teachings on forgiveness? (Matthew 18:21-22)

_____

CHAPTER 24

Knowing Justice and the Church

- **Key Point:** The church's role in promoting justice and righteousness.

- **Discussion Prompt:** How can the church be a beacon of justice in the world?

- **Possible Answers:**

  The church can be a beacon of justice in the world by embodying and promoting the principles of justice as outlined in the Bible. Here are some key points from your document that highlight how the church can achieve this:

- **From your document:**

  1. **Understanding God's Heart for Justice:** Justice is a core attribute of God's character. The Bible often describes God as just and righteous, emphasizing that His actions and judgments are fair and equitable. For example, Deuteronomy 32:4 states, "He is the Rock, his works are perfect, and all his ways are just. A faithful God who does no wrong, upright and just is he".

  2. **Moral Foundation:** The Bible offers a moral framework for human behavior, with justice being a key component of this framework. It calls for fair treatment of all individuals, protection of the vulnerable, and accountability for wrongdoing. This is evident in passages like Micah 6:8, which states, "He has shown you, O mortal, what is good. And what does the Lord require of you? To act justly and to love mercy

and to walk humbly with your God."

3. **Social Justice**: The Bible advocates for social justice, urging believers to care for the poor, the oppressed, and the marginalized. This theme is prevalent in the teachings of the prophets and in the ministry of Jesus. For instance, Isaiah 1:17 instructs, "Learn to do right; seek justice. Defend the oppressed. Take up the cause of the fatherless; plead the case of the widow".

4. **Practical Steps**: To practice biblical justice, the church can:

5. **Educate and Raise Awareness**: Educate community members about their rights and the importance of justice. Awareness campaigns can help people understand the significance of justice and how they can contribute to it.

6. **Engage with the Community**: Encourage active participation in community activities and decision-making processes. When people are involved, they are more likely to advocate for justice and hold authorities accountable.

7. **Support Marginalized Groups**: Provide support and resources to marginalized and vulnerable groups. This can include legal aid, social services, and economic opportunities to help them overcome systemic barriers.

By understanding and using these principles, the church can work towards creating a just and equitable world that reflects God's character and intentions for humanity.

How is equity related to righteousness in Proverbs?
(Proverbs 16:11 ESV)

_____

What does the Bible say about equity in recompense? (Romans 12:20 ESV)

What does the Bible say about showing partiality in judgment? (Deuteronomy 1:17 ESV)

What does the Old Testament law say about equal punishment? (Exodus 21:24-25 ESV)

How does the Bible advise dealing with debt and the poor? (Leviticus 25:35 ESV)

What does the New Testament say about equal punishment? (Matthew 5:38-40 ESV)

How are the Israelites instructed to treat foreigners? (Leviticus 19:34 ESV)

CHAPTER 25

Knowing Equity

- *Key Point:* The relationship between equity, righteousness, and justice in the Bible.

- *Discussion Prompt:* How can we ensure equity in our treatment of others?

- *Possible Answers:*

  Ensuring equity in our treatment of others involves several key principles and actions. Here are some insights from your document:

  From your document:

  1. *Education and Awareness:* Educate community members about their rights and the importance of justice. Awareness campaigns can help people understand the significance of justice and how they can contribute to it.

  2. *Community Engagement:* Encourage active participation in community activities and decision-making processes. When people are involved, they are more likely to advocate for justice and hold authorities accountable.

  3. *Support for Marginalized Groups:* Provide support and resources to marginalized and vulnerable groups. This can include legal aid, social services, and economic opportunities to help them overcome systemic barriers.

  4. *Compassion and Empathy:* Act with compassion and empathy towards others. Treat everyone with the same respect and kindness you desire.

5. Advocating for Justice: *Stand up for the oppressed and marginalized, ensuring that their voices are heard and their rights are protected. This can include activism, legal advocacy, and community organizing.*

By implementing these steps, we can work towards creating a just and equitable world that reflects the principles of fairness and justice.

What does the Bible say about partiality in court? (Deuteronomy 16:19 ESV)

_____

How does God view diverse weights and measures?
(Proverbs 20:10 ESV)

_____

What does the Bible say about treating others as we'd like to be treated? (Matthew 7:12 ESV)

_____

What does Proverbs say about favoring the rich?
(Proverbs 22:16 ESV)

_____

What does the Bible say about justice? (Isaiah 1:17 ESV)

_____

How are believers instructed to regard others? (Philippians 2:3 ESV)

_____

CHAPTER 26

Knowing How to Be Like God

- **Key Point:** *Responding to the needs of the poor and acting justly.*

- **Discussion Prompt:** *What are some practical ways we can be like God in our pursuit of justice?*

- **Possible Answers:**

  Pursuing justice in a way that reflects divine principles can be both inspiring and challenging. Here are some practical ways to embody these principles in our daily lives:

  1. **Show Compassion and Empathy**: *Just as God shows compassion, we can strive to understand and empathize with others, especially those who are marginalized or suffering. This means actively listening to their stories and offering support.*

  2. **Seek Truth and Fairness**: *Upholding truth and fairness in all our dealings is crucial. This involves being honest, transparent, and ensuring that our actions and decisions are just and equitable.*

  3. **Advocate for the Vulnerable**: *Stand up for those who cannot stand up for themselves. This could mean advocating for the rights of the poor, the oppressed, and those who face injustice.*

  4. **Practice Forgiveness**: *While seeking justice, it's also important to practice forgiveness. This doesn't mean ignoring wrongdoing, but rather addressing*

it with a spirit of reconciliation and healing.

5. **Promote Peace**: Work towards resolving conflicts and promoting peace in your community. This can involve mediation, dialogue, and fostering understanding among different groups.

6. **Live with Integrity**: Ensure that your actions align with your values and principles. Integrity builds trust and sets a strong example for others to follow.

7. **Engage in Community Service**: Actively participate in community service and social justice initiatives. This hands-on approach can make a tangible difference in the lives of others.

By incorporating these practices into our lives, we can strive to reflect divine justice and contribute to a more just and compassionate world.

What does the Bible say about responding to the needs of the poor in times of crisis? (Leviticus 25:35 (ESV)

_____

How does the Bible depict justice and righteousness in society? (Psalm 89:14 (ESV)

_____

How does the Lord view unjust scales or measures? (Proverbs 11:1 (ESV)

_____

How should we respond when we see injustice? (Isaiah 1:17 (ESV)

_____

What does the Bible say about partiality in judgment? (Leviticus 19:15 (ESV)

_____

In times of crisis, what attitude should we have towards our resources? (Matthew 5:42 (ESV)

_____

CHAPTER 27

Knowing Justice in the Power of the Cross

- **Key Point:** *The cross of Christ as a demonstration of God's love and justice.*

- **Discussion Prompt:** *How does the cross influence our understanding of justice?*

- **Possible Answers:**

  The cross profoundly influences our understanding of justice by highlighting the intersection of divine justice and mercy. Here are some key points from your document that elaborate on this concept:

- **From your document:**

  - **Divine Nature:** *Justice is a core attribute of God's character. The Bible often describes God as just and righteous, emphasizing that His actions and judgments are fair and*

    equitable. For example, Deuteronomy 32:4 states, "He is the Rock, his works are perfect, and all his ways are just. A faithful God who does no wrong, upright and just is he".

  - **Moral Foundation:** *The Bible offers a moral framework for human behavior, with justice being a key component of this framework. It calls for fair treatment of all individuals, protection of the vulnerable, and accountability for wrongdoing. This is evident in passages like Micah 6:8, which states, "He has shown you, O mortal, what is good. And what does the Lord require of you? To act justly and to love mercy* and to walk humbly with your God."

- ○ **Social Justice**: The Bible advocates for social justice, urging believers to care for the poor, the oppressed, and the marginalized. This theme is prevalent in the teachings of the prophets and in the ministry of Jesus. For instance, Isaiah 1:17 instructs, "Learn to do right; seek justice. Defend the oppressed. Take up the cause of the fatherless; plead the case of the widow".

- ○ These aspects highlight why justice is a central theme in the Bible, reflecting God's character, guiding moral conduct, advocating for social equity, promoting restoration, and offering an eternal hope.

How does the cross of Christ demonstrate both God's love and wrath? (John 3:16, Romans 5:8, Revelation 19:11-16)

_____

How does the resurrection of Christ affirm God's justice and power over evil? (Acts 17:30-31, Romans 6:5-11, Revelation 20:11-15)

_____

How does the Holy Spirit enable and empower Christians to live justly and righteously? (John 16:8-11, Galatians 5:16-26, Ephesians 5:8-10)

_____

How does the church as the body of Christ reflect God's justice and grace to the world? (Matthew 5:13-16, Ephesians 2:11-22, 1 Peter 2:9-12)

_____

How does the church as the bride of Christ anticipate God's final judgment and restoration? (Matthew 25:31-46, Revelation 21:1-8, Revelation 22:12-17)

_____

How should Christians respond to injustice and oppression in their own contexts and cultures? (Luke 10:25-37, Romans 12:9-21, Philippians 2:1-11)

_____

CHAPTER 28

Knowing Crisis Response

- **Key Point:** *Biblical examples of responding to crises.*

- **Discussion Prompt:** *How can we apply these examples to our own crisis responses?*

- **Possible Answers:**

  To apply the examples from your document to your own crisis responses, you can follow these steps:

  1. **Understand the Core Principles**: *The document emphasizes the importance of justice, righteousness, and compassion. These principles should be at the heart of your crisis response strategies. For instance, ensuring fair treatment and protection of the vulnerable can guide your actions during a crisis.*

  2. **Promote Education and Awareness**: *Educate your team and community members about their rights and the importance of justice. Awareness campaigns can help people understand the significance of justice and how they can contribute to it.*

  3. **Engage with the Community**: *Encourage active participation in community activities and decision-making processes. When people are involved, they are more likely to advocate for justice and hold authorities accountable.*

  4. **Support Marginalized Groups**: *Provide support and resources to marginalized and vulnerable groups. This can include legal aid, social services, and economic*

opportunities to help them overcome systemic barriers.

5. **Advocate for Justice**: *Stand up for the oppressed and marginalized, ensuring that their voices are heard and their rights are protected. This can include activism, legal advocacy, and community organizing.*

6. **Reflect on Your Actions**: *Regularly examine your thoughts and motives through self-reflection and prayer. This helps identify any deceitful tendencies and seek guidance to overcome them.*

By integrating these principles and actions into your crisis response strategies, you can create a more just and equitable approach that aligns with the values highlighted in your document.

When Jonah was in the belly of the fish, what was his response? (Jonah 2:1-9 ESV)

_____

How did Job respond to the devastating news of losing his family and property?

(Job 1:20-21ESV)

_____

What did the Lord instruct the Israelites to do when faced with the crisis of the advancing Egyptian army at the Red Sea? (Exodus 14:16 ESV)

_____

How did David react when he heard of Saul's death? (2 Samuel 1:11-12 ESV)

_____

When King Hezekiah was told he would die from his illness, how did he respond? (2 Kings 20:2-3ESV)

_____

How did Mordecai and the Jews in Susa react to King Ahasuerus's decree to destroy the Jews? (Esther 4:1-3 ESV)

_____

When Peter saw Jesus walking on the water, he began to sink, what did he do? (Matthew 14:30 ESV)

_____

Bibliography

[1] denverjournal.denverseminary.edu and preachingsource.com

[2] azquotes.com and goodreads.com

[3] Robert W. Lee, descendant of Confederate General Robert E. Lee, author, "A Sin By Any Other Name." NPR Interview on April 2, 2019.

[4] The Christian Watchman & Reflector 19th Century Boston Baptist Newspaper: Article by Rev. C.H. Spurgeon, September 27, 1860. Article by Rev. C.H. Spurgeon, August 23, 1860.

[5] https://www.spurgeon.org/resource-library/blog-entries/the-reason-why-america-burned-spurgeons-sermons-and-sought-to-kill-him/

[6] Why Social Justice is not Biblical Justice by Scott David Allen

[7] God's Justice vs. Human Justice by Morgan Guyton

[8] thewitness.org

[9] Grand Canyon University – Theology Thursday: Justice in the Old Testament

[10] Biblegateway.com

[11] Biblestudytools.com

[12] Lifehopeandtruth.com and biblestudytools.com

[13] Christianity.com

[14] Churchgists.com

[15] Praywithconfidence.com

[16] gsdrc.org and universalhumanrightsindex.org

[17] Bible.knowing-jesus.com and biblestudytools.com

[18] Bible.knowing-Jesus.com and bing.com

Disclaimer

This document is intended to provide a biblical perspective on justice, which is rooted in God's character and His will for His people. It does not address specific legal issues or cases, nor does it advocate for any form of retribution or violence against those who commit injustice. The reader is advised to consult other sources for such matters, and to exercise discernment and wisdom in applying the principles of biblical justice to their own context.

Systematic Bible Study Section

Here's a structured approach to help create a Systematic Bible Study.

1. **Introduction**
   - **Purpose**: Explain the purpose of the study guide and what participants can expect to learn.
   - **Definition**: Define systematic theology and its importance in understanding biblical justice.

2. **Foundational Concepts**
   - **Justice in the Bible**: Provide an overview of how justice is portrayed in both the Old and New Testaments.
   - **Key Attributes of God**: Discuss God's justice as one of His key attributes, supported by scripture (e.g., Deuteronomy 32:4, Psalm 89:14).

3. Biblical Passages on Justice
   - **Old Testament**: Explore passages such as Micah 6:8, Isaiah 1:17, and Amos 5:24.
   - **New Testament**: Examine teachings of Jesus and the apostles on justice, such as Matthew 23:23, Luke 4:18-19, and James 1:27.

4. Systematic Theology Framework
   - **Doctrine of God**: How God's nature and character define justice.
   - **Doctrine of Humanity**: Human dignity and the call to justice.
   - **Doctrine of Sin**: How sin distorts justice and creates injustice.

- **Doctrine of Salvation**: Redemption and restoration of justice through Christ.
- **Doctrine of the Church**: The role of the church in promoting justice.
- **Eschatology**: The ultimate fulfillment of justice in God's kingdom.

5. **Practical Application**
   - **Personal Reflection**: Encourage participants to reflect on their own lives and how they can pursue justice.
   - **Community Engagement**: Discuss ways to engage in justice within the community, such as advocacy, service, and support for marginalized groups.

6. **Discussion Questions**
   - What does biblical justice mean to you?
   - How can we reflect God's justice in our daily lives?
   - What are some contemporary issues of justice that the church should address?

7. **Additional Resources**
   - Books: Recommend books like "Knowing God's Truth" by Jon Nielson[1] and "Systematic Theology" by Wayne Grudem[2].
   - Online Courses: Suggest online courses such as those offered by BiblicalTraining.org[3].

8. **Conclusion**
   - Summarize key points and encourage ongoing study and application of biblical justice.

Purpose of the Study Guide

The purpose of this Bible study guide is to provide a comprehensive understanding of the systematic theology of justice as presented in the Bible. Participants will explore the nature of God's justice, how it is reflected in His character, and how it should be manifested in our lives and communities. This study aims to deepen your theological knowledge and inspire practical application of biblical justice in everyday situations.

WHAT PARTICIPANTS CAN EXPECT TO LEARN

1. **Foundational Understanding**: Gain a solid foundation in systematic theology and its relevance to justice.

2. **Biblical Insights**: Discover key biblical passages that highlight God's justice and His call for us to act justly.

3. **Theological Framework**: Understand how different doctrines (e.g., the nature of God, humanity, sin, salvation, the church, and eschatology) interconnect to form a cohesive view of justice.

4. **Practical Application**: Learn practical ways to apply biblical principles of justice in personal and community contexts.

5. **Discussion and Reflection**: Engage in meaningful discussions and reflections that challenge and encourage growth in understanding and living out justice.

Definition of Systematic Theology

Systematic theology is a branch of Christian theology that seeks to formulate an orderly, rational, and coherent account of the doctrines of the Christian faith. It involves summarizing and synthesizing the teachings of the Bible on various topics to create a comprehensive and unified understanding of God's truth[12].

IMPORTANCE IN UNDERSTANDING BIBLICAL JUSTICE

Systematic theology is crucial for understanding biblical justice because it helps us:

1. **Clarify Concepts**: By organizing and defining theological concepts, systematic theology provides clarity on what justice means from a biblical perspective. This includes understanding God's nature as just and righteous, and how His justice is reflected in His actions and commands[3].

2. **Integrate Teachings**: It integrates teachings from different parts of the Bible, showing how justice is a consistent theme throughout Scripture. This holistic approach helps us see the bigger picture of God's plan for justice in the world[4].

3. **Address Contemporary Issues**: Systematic theology applies biblical principles to contemporary issues, helping us navigate modern challenges with a biblically grounded understanding of justice. This is essential for addressing social, economic, and political injustices in a way that aligns with God's will[5].

4. **Guide Practical Application**: It provides a framework for applying biblical justice in our lives and communities. By understanding the theological foundations of justice, we can better pursue justice in practical ways, such as advocating for the oppressed and promoting fairness and equity[3].

Justice in the Bible

OLD TESTAMENT

In the Old Testament, justice is a fundamental attribute of God and a central theme throughout the scriptures. Here are some key aspects:

1. **God's Character**: Justice is intrinsic to God's nature. He is described as just and righteous, showing no partiality and accepting no bribes (Deuteronomy 10:17-18).

2. **Creation and Imago Dei**: The concept of justice is rooted in the creation narrative, where humans are made in the image of God (Genesis 1:26-27). This implies that all humans have inherent dignity and worth, deserving of just treatment[1].

3. **Laws and Commandments**: The Mosaic Law includes numerous commands to ensure justice, especially for the vulnerable, such as widows, orphans, and foreigners (Exodus 22:21-24, Deuteronomy 24:17-18). The Year of Jubilee (Leviticus 25) is a notable example, designed to restore economic balance and prevent perpetual poverty[2].

4. **Prophetic Calls for Justice**: Prophets like Isaiah, Amos, and Micah frequently called Israel to act justly and condemned social injustices. For instance, Micah 6:8 emphasizes doing justice, loving mercy, and walking humbly with God[1].

NEW TESTAMENT

In the New Testament, the concept of justice expands to include themes of restoration and reconciliation:

1. **Jesus' Ministry**: Jesus' mission was deeply rooted in justice. He proclaimed good news to the poor, freedom for the prisoners, and recovery of sight for the blind (Luke 4:18-19). His teachings often emphasized justice, mercy, and faithfulness (Matthew 23:23)[3].

2. **Kingdom of God**: Jesus' teachings on the Kingdom of God highlight a society where justice prevails. The Beatitudes (Matthew 5:6) bless those who hunger and thirst for justice[4].

3. Parables and Teachings: Parables like the Good Samaritan (Luke 10:25-37) and the Prodigal Son (Luke 15:11-32) illustrate principles of justice, mercy, and reconciliation[5].

4. **Apostolic Teachings**: The apostles continued to emphasize justice. James, for example, speaks against favoritism and calls for caring for orphans and widows (James 1:27, 2:1-9)[6].

SUMMARY

Justice in the Bible is portrayed as a reflection of God's character and a mandate for His people. It encompasses fair treatment, protection of the vulnerable, and the pursuit of righteousness. In the New Testament, justice is further enriched by themes of mercy, reconciliation, and the establishment of God's Kingdom on earth.

Key Attributes of God: Justice

God's justice is one of His essential and infinite attributes, reflecting His moral righteousness and fairness. Here are some key points supported by scripture:

1. **God's Nature and Character**:

   o **Deuteronomy 32:4**: "He is the Rock, his works are perfect, and all his ways are just. A faithful God who does no wrong, upright and just is he." This verse highlights that God's actions are inherently just and perfect, emphasizing His unwavering righteousness[1].

   o Psalm 89:14: "Righteousness and justice are the foundation of your throne; love and faithfulness go before you." This scripture underscores that justice is foundational to God's rule and governance, intertwined with His righteousness and love[1].

2. **Impartiality and Fairness**:

   o Acts 10:34-35: "Then Peter began to speak: 'I now realize how true it is that God does not show favoritism but accepts from every nation the one who fears him and does what is right.'" God's justice is impartial, extending to all who seek Him and live righteously[2].

   o Romans 2:6-11: Paul explains that God "will repay each person according to what they have done," and that "there is no favoritism with God." This passage reinforces the idea that God's justice is fair and equitable[2].

3. **Vindication and Protection**:

   ○ Psalm 103:6: "The Lord works righteousness and justice for all the oppressed." God is portrayed as a defender of the oppressed, ensuring that justice is served on their behalf[3].

   ○ Isaiah 61:8: "For I, the Lord, love justice; I hate robbery and wrongdoing." This verse reflects God's deep commitment to justice and His opposition to all forms of injustice[3].

4. **Judgment and Reward**:

   ○ **Revelation 20:12**: "And I saw the dead, great and small, standing before the throne, and books were opened. Another book was opened, which is the book of life. The dead were judged according to what they had done as recorded in the books." This passage illustrates God's ultimate justice in the final judgment, where everyone is held accountable for their actions[4].

Summary

God's justice is a core attribute that permeates His nature and actions. It is characterized by His perfect righteousness, impartiality, protection of the oppressed, and fair judgment. Understanding God's justice helps us appreciate His moral perfection and guides us in living justly according to His will.

Would you like to explore any other attributes of God or delve deeper into specific scriptures? [5]: Crosswalk [3]: Bible Study Tools [2]: Bible Gateway [1]: Bible Hub [4]: The Witness

www.ingramcontent.com/pod-product-compliance
Lightning Source LLC
Chambersburg PA
CBHW070639130626
46555CB00006B/2625